Seclusion

By

Twila Nicholas

Order this book online at www.trafford.com
or email orders@trafford.com

Most Trafford titles are also available at major online book retailers.

Printed in Victoria, BC, Canada.

ISBN: 978-1-4269-2640-2 (sc)

*Our mission is to efficiently provide the world's finest, most comprehensive book publishing
service, enabling every author to experience success. To find out how to publish your book, your
way, and have it available worldwide, visit us online at www.trafford.com*

Trafford rev. 2/11/2010

 www.trafford.com

North America & international
toll-free: 1 888 232 4444 (USA & Canada)
phone: 250 383 6864 ♦ fax: 812 355 4082

Liquid Glass

I dine on liquid glass,
Blue velvet,
Dreaming,
Waves are in sequence.
Above crystal waters,
Below majestic mountains.
Late summer breeze;
Fantasy fills the day.
Embracing simplicity;
Imagination is born.
Rippling velvet,
Dancing;
Above crystal waters.
Unwind and breath,
With crystal adorn,
Blue velvet,
I dine on liquid glass.

2008

Calm

Waves crash against the shore,
Gulls bath in the sun.
The coast line is clear,
Taste the salt on the breeze.

Thoughts are free,
A vessel appears.
Toward port it creeps,
The end of a journey is near.

Gulls bath in the sun,
A warm summer breeze,
Calm is the day,
Waves crash against the shore.

2001

Ambitious spirit

Ambitious spirit
A free spirit.
No expectations
No consequences.
The future,
Future is the only horizon,
Endeavors with no boundaries.
A strong endurance
Hope for tomorrow.
Challenge is a goal,
Achievement is sought.
Life keeps flowing,
The ambitious keep moving.
Expectations improving
Human strength is divine.
Faltering is not an option,
Failing is not a thought.
The future is the only horizon
Endeavors with no boundaries.
No expectations,
No consequences.
A free spirit,
Ambitious spirit.

The Hypocrite

A hypocrite,
A saint.
With cunning wit,
One face they both paint.

The alter of good,
The threshold of sin.
No room for innocents,
The difference is thin.

Caress the bible
Tell a lie.
No one is reliable,
Another chance to connive.

The ending is all the same,
A hypocrite is fate,
A continuing game,
Sainthood is to late.

A hypocrite,
A saint,
With cunning wit,
One face they both paint.

Somewhere Unknown

I am somewhere unknown,
The road is not clearly shown.
Where is here?
I feel no fear.

I try to think.
All I did was blink.
Follow the signs
Traveled a white line.

Where am I?
Somewhere under a foreign sky.
Nowhere is a place,
My steps I begin to trace.

No worry,
The direction is blurry.
Figure this out,
I am not a lout.

I know where I am going,
Even though
Not sure what I am doing.
The road is not clearly shown,
I am somewhere unknown.

August 2000

Waking Dawn

Waking dawn
A new day.
Overwhelmed with emotion,
Glistening spirit.
The world awakens
In the morning mist.

Waking dawn
A journey has begun
Today is seen
In the new sun.

September 14, 2000

Lullaby

My devotion;
My love.
My life,
My sweet lullaby.

Soothing is the sound
Soothing is the touch.
Life's eternal devotion,
Loves soft lullaby.

Rare is the gift,
Rare is the fate.
Given by heaven,
Loves true creation.

Human is feeling,
Human is living.
Living is eternal
Loves soft lullaby.

My devotion,
My love.
My life,
My sweet lullaby.

The Lion

A lion I see,
I begin to wonder
What does he want with me.

Closer he appears
Face to face
He lingers near.

Feline eyes appear in front of me,
A child's face
My own reflection I see.

Within the night
The lion roams
Appearing within my sight.

The lion is eternity,
A part of me,
A salvation that will set me free.

In a felines eyes I see me,
Bind together as one,
A lion I see.

1994

Needed

Needed
Security,
An inner freedom.
Acceptance
A need
Everyone dreams.
Helping,
Just a smile will do.
Comfort
A place
Everyone needs.

Political

Dreary morning,
Hear an eerie sound.
A sudden warning,
The world seems to frown.

Dusk is at an end,
Battalions begin to flock,
A nation is weaken,
The world begins to rock.

Tension plays with time,
Rare is innocent and true,
Anxiety draws a line,
Truth is found in a certain few.

The recovery is long,
Casualties in magnitude.
Political view is wrong,
Thousands are not a few.

2003

Desert Road

I feel you drift away,
Brave hero
During the night.
Travel toward foreign shores,
Far from home.

With courage strong,
You face the foe.
Never looking back,
Down a desert road.

Valor is your shield,
In a world led astray.
Toward a foreign war,
Unknown land you stay.

The strong will not falter,
Nor give in.
Keep marching,
To the same steady rhythm.

The brave stand proud and true,
One last heroes deed,
During the night,
On a foreign battle field you find the end,
I feel you drift away.

September 2003

I was asked to write a poem about a Door

I was asked to write a poem about a door,
I thought about a rectangle,
Then,
I thought about the floor.
Stare at the geometrical angle.
I slammed it shut,
Then,
I opened it.
The wood had been cut,
The frame did not fit.
I believe it impossible,
I thought it would be a bore.
Over all,
It is a nice obstacle
I was asked to write a poem about a door.

Intimacy

A noise within the dark,
A startling hark.
A figure appears,
Lovers voice whispers in my ear.

A moment of peace,
Let affection ease.
The moment is mine,
Let go of time.

Passionate thought,
Intimacy is sought.
A voice speaks,
Intimacy seeks.

Glisten

Glisten, Glisten
The fresh fallen dew.
Ray of reflection
Shines
Within the morning hues.

Sleepy eyes
Wake
Reach within the sky.
Sea of maroon,
Blossoms
In the world before noon.

Glisten, glisten
The fresh fallen dew.
Ray of reflection
Shines
Within a day of new.

Screaming

A mirror shatters
A horrible scream
Emotions are tattered
The source of life is a flowing stream.

Withered and worn,
A mess this is.
A soul is torn,
A sadden complacent bliss.

A scream is heard,
Tattered flesh lays on the ground.
The sound of the black bird is heard,
The source of life is sound.

Don't Look At Me

Don't look at me,
I am on a path of self discovery.
Untidy is my life,
The road has been a long strife.

Don't look at me
I am searching for endless possibilities.
I have gone through many a phase,
Soon I will find the right place.

Don't look at me,
I am trying to find life's golden key.
To young they say,
I will be older some day.

Don't look at me,
One day I will see.
I still have lessons to be learned,
Respect is something earned.

Don't look at me,
I am on a path of self discovery.
One day I will trade my youth,
I will be just like you.

Close Enough to Care

One moment
Hidden emotion.
Love is in my grasp.
Close enough to touch,
Close enough to care.

Silence
Unspoken word,
Hidden love that is unknown.
Close enough to touch
Close enough to care.

One moment
Uttering devotion
Love is in my grasp
Close enough to touch
Close enough to care.

The Vipers Nest

Down by a river,
The soul will shiver.
In a corrupt town,
No one can sleep sound.

Deception unwinds
A foul odor of the strongest kind.
Corruption is deep,
Within the veins it will seep.

A place of sin,
The devil grins.
Murder and greed,
Deception is a simple deed.

Deception never rest,
In the vipers nest.
No one sleeps sound,
In a corrupt town.

The Call

A raspy voice calls,
As darkness falls.
Gray, white, and brown;
Feathers tumble toward the ground.
Small game run in fright,
Screeching away from sight.
Something is watching me,
Perched from on the roof.
The creatures lets out a scream,
Chasing me toward the distant stream.
Darkness falls,
A raspy voice calls.

Follow Grace with Sin

She is a mystery
A long ancient history.
Secrets kept,
Unseen tears are wept.

Deep is the soul
Yearning to be whole.
Many broken ends,
She faces the critical winds.

Memories she buries,
A lot of burdens she carries.
Weary is the heart,
Whimsical with adventure she departs.

Living life on a whim,
Follow grace with sin.
A long ancient history,
She becomes a mystery.

The Answer

A question,
The gentle voice asks.
Round eyes appear,
A complexing task.

I raise my head,
I glance her way.
She shyly treads,
Then begins to say.

The one question that baffles all,
Searching for a simple word.
The question that makes us stall,
The answer is absurd.

Untitled I

Fading is time,
Fading are memories.
Forgotten mistakes,
A becoming familiarity.
Distant,
Age,
Numbness the hands feel.
Changing
A stranger I appear to be.

Fading is the memories,
Fading is yesterday.
Mistakes I made
A becoming familiarity.
Distant,
Age,
Numbness the emotions feel.
Changing,
Time has appeared.

A Confession

A confession
The words of truth
Relieved
The body can breath.
A confession
The words of love.
Lifting the clouds of fear,
Erasing the doubt as it appears.
A confession
Eternal salvation,
Saving sanity,
The words of truth appear.

Hallway

A hall of windows,
This is where I walk.
Crimson curtains sway,
In the breeze of the day.
Wooden floors,
White walls,
A row of ancient doors.
The breeze howls has it strays,
I continue to walk
Down the ancient hallway.

Gentle Canary

Sing gentle canary,
Stories you carry.
Appalachian wind,
A family legacy that never ends.

A stained face,
A coal miners grace.
Food on the table,
Ancestry label.

Buried in a dark hole,
Only the bravest of souls.
Dust fills the lungs,
Where only a certain few belong.

The earth creeks and moans,
Daylight is never shown.
The bowels shake,
Endless nerves rake.

Simple is a coal miners life,
The rich mans never ending strife.
Dirty the faces appear,
A life without fear.

A lonely coal miners story,
A dark purgatory.
The young turn into the old,
A legacy that never folds.

Appalachian wind,
An ancestry that will never end.
Tomorrow the stories will carry,
Within the gentle Canary.

Book of Life

Book of life
Give me salvation.
A creation of strife
Mortal soul hangs in levitation.

The alter of redemption I kneel,
Grievance of human sin.
Whisper a prayer to heal,
Forgiveness in the end.

Searching for advice,
Remorse shows the tears.
A sin committed twice,
Turmoil fought through out the years.

I search for gods face,
A mortal souls strife.
Finding immortal grace
Book of life.

The Day is Whole

Resting on a grassy green knoll,
The country unfolds.
Twilight begins to fall,
West Virginia nightingale calls.

A tractor strolls across the fields,
When the sun begins to yield.
The kadid grows loud,
Nature is the only crowd.

Another day withers away,
The farmer calls it a day.
Waiting for the crickets sound,
My heart is bound.

Twilight begins to fall,
West Virginia nightingale calls.
Another day becomes whole,
Resting on a grassy green knoll.

Another Possession

A lost obsession
Another possession.
A porcelain ornament,
Our love has been long spent.

You walk away,
Then reappear one day.
Vanish without a call,
I am trapped against a wall.

You say you need me,
You need to be free.
Endless game you play,
Again you stray.

I am ready to quit,
I can no longer resist.
A lost obsession,
Another possession.

Imperfection

Self-esteem is in shreds,
Facing foes I dread.
The past only judge,
I still hold a grudge.

Only perfection,
Starved of affection.
A miserable creation,
I want no affiliation.

Disgust bully,
I never understood truly.
Actions are vile,
Imperfection is my style.

Words can be cruel,
Hatred has no rules.
Imperfection is yelled at me,
As an outcast I am free.

Done

Oblivion, oblivion,
A world with no end.
Done is done,
Not returning again.

A chapter I close,
From a place that I loath.
Done is done,
Not returning again.

The heart is breaking,
My mind is still shaking,
Done is done,
Not returning again.

Oblivion, oblivion,
A world with no end.
Done is done
Not returning again.

The Sun

Cocoon of warmth,
This is what I feel.
The scent of the earth,
The moment is real.

Cocoon of warmth,
Bathing in the sun.
The scent of the earth,
The moment is undone.

The Fawn

A doe,
Thin and frail,
Stumbles,
Leaving prints in the snow.
She stops,
Then looks my way.
I met her gaze,
Helpless and afraid.
The silence
Broken
Coyotes thick on her trail.
She lets out a wail,
Death becomes her end,
Natures bitter end.
Nature,
A way of life,
Love is a sacrifice.
I look down,
I glimpse prints in the snow,
I follow.
Soon
Laying at my feet,
Shivering and alone,
A newborn doe.

The Gathering Of Essence

Devotion is clear,
A wedding day draws near.
Purity finds a place,
In the silence of the day.
The bell begins to chime,
Time appears,
The gathering of essence draws near.

Devotion is clear,
As sensuality draws near.
Forgiveness finds a place,
In the silence of the day.
The bell begins to chime,
Elegance appears.
The gathering of essence draws near.

Tumble

She takes a tumble,
Just another stumble.
She picks herself up,
Starts from the beginning again.

She lets out a low cry,
Then she sighs.
She slowly walks across the floor.
As she holds onto the door.

She holds her head high,
Humiliation hides behind her pride.
She begins to tumble,
Just another stumble.

Untitled II

Chime,
Wind chime,
Chime.
The winds of change I can feel today.
Chime,
As we dream for the war to be done.

Chime
Wind chime
Chime.
Bring good news today.
Chime,
A new era has begun.

Chime
Wind chime
Chime.
The winds of change I can feel today.
Chime,
As we dream for the war to be done.

Abandon

The floor boards creek,
As curiosity seeks.
Dirt between the wooden grooves.
Dust bunnies move.
Abandon house,
The home of a curious mouse.
Interior in ruins,
A habitat for restless raccoons.
Tree branch quivers,
The body shivers.
Mysterious manor of old,
Once worth ten thousand gold.
The floor boards creek,
As curiosity creeps.

I Will Wait

I will wait
Wait for you ate heavens gate.
I will wait,
Even if you are late.

Love is my journey,
Learning
Feeling,
Knowing you.

Love is my desire,
A journey I will make to find you.
Eternity,
I want to spend with you.

I will wait,
Even if you are late.
I will wait,
Wait for you at heavens gate.

Untitled III

Rolling; rolling
Storm clouds appear in the hemisphere.
The thunder rumbles,
The rain is almost here.

Rolling, rolling,
A dark angel appears,
The thunder rumbles,
Death is almost here.

If I Could Tell

Time can say nothing,
Except,
I told you so.
Time,
Only knows the price,
Of the debts we must pay.
If we shall know wisdom
When it is given.
Time,
Whispers,
If I could tell you,
I would let you know.

Time can say nothing
Except
I told you so.
Time,
If we shall overcome our faults,
Humble our pride.
If we shall stop judging others,
Before we judge ourselves.
Time
Whispers
If I could tell you,
I would let you know.

Time can say nothing,
Except
I told you so.
Time,

If we will recognize love,
Before our time is to late.
If we should learn from our mistakes,
Before forgiveness is to late.
Time
Whispers,
If I could tell you
I would let you know.

Time can say nothing,
Except
I told you so.
Time
Only knows,
When to late is to late,
When enough is enough.
If we shall learn to find peace,
Before we destroy ourselves.
Time
Whispers
If I could tell you
I would let you know.

Bitterness

Hospitality slams the door,
Unwanted welcome sign,
No smile at the door.

Looks could kill
Unwanted gesture
Signs of ill-will.

Shunned from a place known,
Talk is cheap,
Rudeness is greatly shown.

Bitterness is in the atmosphere
Time to leave,
Show my back rear.

Isolation

Wrapped in a blanket of solitude
Isolation
Peacefulness.
I hear my thoughts,
I feel my emotions.
I can think,
I can dream.

Wrapped in a blanket of solitude,
Isolation,
I choose not to be found.
I can hear my thoughts,
Simple is the life,
No rat race,
No people,
No strife.

Wrapped in a blanket of solitude,
Isolation,
Alone at last,
Simple is the moment,
I begin to think,
I can dream.

Free

My heart is free
A silent place of decree.
A place where I belong,
The road has been long.

I am home bound,
Happiness is found.
I feel free,
As I am accepted as me.

Years turn to miles,
As time slowly files.
Finding a place within,
Generosity is given.

Toward home I race,
A beautiful place.
A silent place of decree,
My heart is free.

From the Ashes

Rising from the ashes,
Broken and abused,
Her life flashes,
Her body used.

Living is sleeping,
She takes another pill.
Her heart is still weeping,
A slow climb up life's hill.

She treads in shallow water,
The current is strong.
Never again will she falter,
Even when the road is to long.

Days will pass,
Life will soon flash.
This to shall come to pass,
Rising from the ash.

The Mind

The mind
Visions the soul.
Feel the pain,
Anguish,
Hostility raves.

The mind
Foreshadows many things.
Deception,
Truth,
Turmoil it finds.

The mind,
Feels the cry.
Shaken overwhelmed
Behind the eyes,
Within the mind.

The mind,
The problems it brings,
Visions the soul
The emotions it holds,
The conflict will one day set you free.

Cascade

Heaven
I see today
Behind the clouds
Beyond the sun.
The sky open
With rays of yellow flare.
Cascading down
I could only stare.

Heaven
I see today
Mountains engulfed.
In rays of purple and blue,
Sparkles of delight,
Reflecting in crystal hues.

Heaven
I see today.
Behind the clouds
Beyond the sun.
Rays of yellow flare,
Descended from the sky above.
With arms reached high,
I felt the wings of a dove.

Untitled II

A sea of turqoise blue,
Devotion is mine
A moment of peace,
I see the way.
Serenity
Consumes me,
When hope finds the day.
The scent of you,
Fills my emotions,
Devotion is mine,
A sea of turqouise blue.

Minutes and Memories

I open my eyes and I begin to see.
Who I once was and who I can be.
The minutes roll by,
Days just fly.
I wipe the dust from a old box upon the shelf,
A stranger unto myself.
Snap shots of people I once knew
Time I lost, Time I went through.
The present is all that will be,
One day I will lock away the memories,
And throw away the key.
No one stays the same,
Everyone changes,
Nothing is to blame.
I place a box upon the shelf,
A stranger unto myself.
The minutes roll by,
Days just fly.
I open my eyes and I begin to see,
Who I once was and who I can be.

Tranquility

Whisper a silent prayer
Remove another layer.
A stream of tears are unleashed,
A ships final destination is beached.

The coast line is in ruins,
Souls rest upon the dunes.
Reaching for a higher possibility
Forever living on the shores of tranquility.

Small Steps

The steps are absurd
As I allured.
A sentence stops,
I become lost in thought.
The body of a dancer,
The steps are only fancier.
Color of infusion,
Swirling in confusion.
Spinning and twirling,
The floor is uncurling.
Again,
The small steps begin.
The body becomes wired,
As the mind becomes inspired.

False

False accusation
Look of disgrace.
Unwanted gesture
One person out of place.

False rumor,
Bad reputation.
Cruel tongue,
One persons complication.

False hope,
Whispers loom.
The damage has been done,
One person is doomed.

Garden

Exhaustion consumes me
As I dig another row.
Pull one more weed,
My hard work will soon show.

Plow the ground
I push the rotor tiller,
The motor makes a sound,
I swat at a miller.

A few months the garden will grow,
The hard done.
The harvest has been sow
The garden season has begun.

Summer Wind

I look back upon yesterday,
My heart is on the mend,
I look at the path I walk today,
I feel the summer wind.

I see the reflection of you in the mountain stream.
I can feel you near.
Open my mind to dream,
Your vision is becomes clear.

I walk near the place we shared,
My heart is on the mend.
I lost you in a moment that I dared,
I feel the summer wind.

Memories that I have forgotten,
Loving you is what I had always known.
I think of the golden field often,
Where the winds of yesterday have blown.

I find my strength,
My heart is on the mend.
My hearts desire was once at arms length,
I feel the summer wind.

The Drums

Beating, Beating
I hear the drums beating for me.
Waiting, waiting
My love waits for me.
My blood is burning.
I feel you pulsating in my veins.
I desire that you set me free
I can feel your breath upon my skin,
I desire that you set me free.
My blood is burning for the need of you.
Waiting, waiting,
My love waits for me.
Beating, beating,
I hear the drums beating for me.

Lily's War

Precious lily
Let the tears flow,
No need to shut them behind a prideful door.
Love is not the end,
The soul is not condemned.
Pray for strength
Over come this dreadful battle.
Let the tears flow,
As you try to carry on.
Feelings are numb,
The battle has just begun.
You will not lose this war.

Gentle lily
Grieving,
You lay at gods door.
Do not lose hope,
Let your tears flow.
Pray for strength
Over come this dreadful battle.
Let the tears flow,
A quiet prayer you whisper on.
Emptiness overcomes.
The battle has just begun,
You will not lose this war.

Precious lily
Let the tears flow.
Love is not the end,
An angel god will send.
Pray for strength

Over come this dreadful battle.
Let the tears flow,
Don't shut them behind a prideful door.
Feelings have become numb,
As the battle has begun.
You will not lose this war.

Scandal

A scandal goes down,
Everyone knows.
What goes around comes around,
Bad judgment shows.

Nothing is discreet
A simple commotion,
Gossip on the street,
Wheels of exaggeration are in motion.

Idiotic manifestation,
A persons reputation is torn down.
Lack of communication,
A scandal goes down.

Dizzy

The room is spinning
I feel ill,
The air is to warm.
My skin is flushed,
A sugar rush.
The floor is unsteady
I feel ill
I feel dizzy.

Somber

Somber
Is the tone today.
Sleep
Sleep the day away.
Lazy,
Lazy the day has been.
Dreary,
Dreary is the sky above.
Watching
Watching the rain fall
Sleep
Sleep the day away.
Somber
Somber is the tone today.

Gentle Grace

Within a child's grace
Innocent shine
Behind a shy face.

Sleeping quietly
Softly breathing
Caressing ever so lightly.

Watching the innocent sleep
Dreaming.
A whimper turns into a weep.

Finding peace
Within securities reach,
The hurt will soon ease.

Gentle embrace
Love endures
Within a child's grace.

The Standing Stone

Among the frozen snow
The winds of sadness blow.
The sun is burning low,
I hear death crow.

I read the name upon the standing stone,
Despair is only known.
God called you home,
I am left standing alone.

The streams no longer flow,
Time moves slow.
Life is not the same,
There is no one to blame.

I read the name upon the standing stone.
Emptiness is only known.
God called you home,
I am left standing alone.

I watched your dreams unfold,
As you slowly grew old.
With love and grace,
Never losing faith.

I read the name upon the standing stone.
Emptiness is only known.
God called you home,
I am left standing alone.

A Liability of Uncertainty

It is time for my ship to sail,
Unmask my veil.
Time to leave,
Ambition I need to unweave.

Unexplored possibilities are deep,
To many stories to keep.
I feel tomorrows breeze,
My spirit begins to breath.

Freedom lays ahead,
Through undiscovered waters I tread.
Where I go, I do not know,
I am searching for tomorrow.

My journey is one of uncertainty,
The human spirit has no liability
Unmask my veil,
It is time for my ship to sail.

Clay Creek

Hot, humid, and hazy;
A fiddle echoes somewhere in the night.
The town seems to be lazy,
The moon shine bright.

The night pushes onward
The water is shallow, but deep,
A coal truck slowly moves forward,
Another hot summers night in Clay Creek.

Storm clouds roll in
As I sit on the porch swing.
The white tails play in the sultry wind.
I hear the blue grass music sing.

The old hound dog bellows,
The water is shallow, but deep.
A train whistles through the hollow,
Another hot summers night in Clay Creek.

Love is Blind

Searching for peace
Into my mind you creep.
A game within my mind,
Love is blind.

I think twice,
As you seep into my mind thrice.
Wrestling with the thought,
A peace of mind is sought.

You make me feel meek
As my feelings toward you grow weak.
You are game within my mind,
Love is blind.

I will not stay,
No matter what you say.
My senses you consume,
Your face still looms.

Searching for peace,
Into my mind you creep.
You are a game within my mind,
Love is blind.

Face

Two faces
A decision
A choice
Which face will appear today.
One with compassion,
Concern and kindness.
Two faces,
A decision
A choice
One with cruelty,
Discontent and scorn.
Which face will appear today.

A Reflection of Creation

A reflection of creation,
Never ending journey.
The elements forum.
Fire of passion,
Waters of tranquility,
Winds of wisdom,
Earths of existents.
Together creation is made,
A cycle forms,
A journey
The elements forum
A reflection of creation.

Untitled V

Knowledge,
A book where fact is found.
Thoughts are place,
Hypothesis are made.

Wisdom
A book of mistakes
Learning from life's journey,
Simply observing.

Untitled VI

Flourish
White dove.
On mended wing
You can fly.

A set back,
It is a common state.
On mended wing
You can fly.

Lift your spirit
White dove
On mended wing
You can fly.

Complicated

Complicated,
Two loves
One loss.
Complicated,
Mysterious is the emotion,
Fumble is the mind.
A difficult decision,
When the heart can't decide.
Complicated
Two loves.
One loss.
Complicated,
A triangle this is,
When love becomes
Complicated.

Lazy Spring Day

Lazy spring day
Kids at play
A robin flies by,
Not a cloud in the sky.

Day dream,
Among by a flowing stream
A hammock in the wind
Visions begin to blend.

Sensual thought,
Peace is sought.
Scent of Jasmine in the air,
Meditate without a care.

Essence

Essence
Sweet essence
Whisper my name
Waiting,
Waiting on a plain.

Essence
Sweet essence
I call out your name,
Feeling
May your presence always remain.

Purity and Sin

Purity and sin
Loving you will be my end.
Concealed by desire,
Sealed by fate.
Asking
Arrives one moment to late.
Pure is my thoughts,
Loving you is my fate.
Sin is my action,
Loving you a moment to late.
Concealed by desire,
Sealed by fate.
Loving you will be my end,
Purity and sin.

Yellow Finch

Yellow finch
Watching me,
Perched on a branch
From the weeping willow tree
A yellow finch sings to me.
The song carries on the wind,
A lovely sound it sends.
The yellow finch I see,
Perched on the weeping willow tree.
The limb begins to bend,
As the song carries on the wind.
From a weeping willow tree
A yellow finch sings to me.

Reunion

The meal is on the table,
Everything seems stable.
When does this thing start,
Cousin Ernie acts smart.

The kids are playing in the water again,
Great aunt Betsy story finally ends.
Cousin Joese is engaged,
Uncle Bob is going to rage.

The ice cream is melting,
Little cousin George is pouting.
Its time to eat and we start to pray,
"I want white meat" I hear aunt Lauren say.

Family reunions create their own tune,
Cousin Mervie wants to leave soon.
The elders speak of growing old,
As we listen to family stories being told.

I Follow You

I follow you,
We run through the evening hue.
Away from here
On the longest day of the year.

A chill in the wind
A silent thought you send.
Sweet compromise,
Feel my anxiety rise.

You show me the way,
We don't delay.
Free will,
Time with you stands still.

Don't slow down,
The moment is sound.
I feel you near me,
Serenity is all I see.

You have my devotion,
The present is no longer in motion.
My love is true,
I follow you.

Untitled VII

The time is growing late
The sky is growing dark.
I can not stay,
I must depart.

The stars twinkle above,
As I say good night.
Please, don't say this is love,
My feelings are what I fight.

The clock strikes one,
My feelings grow.
This is an affair I can't condone,
I must go.

One more moment,
One last time.
You softly whisper,
"One day you will be mine"

You Journey Home

You journey home
Weary knight.
An exhausting war
You have endured.
The road has been long,
A trying road to victory.
You have traveled
Toward destinations with no end.
Valor,
You still seek.
Head held high
With patriotic pride.
One last breath
You fight.
With a strong will
You don't give in.

Unveil your armor,
Time to rest.
Strong and steadfast
You never falter.
A mortal shell that is broken,
You struggle to carry on.
Angels are calling,
Your soul will soon be home.
The battle is done,
The war will soon be won.
With courage,
You fight to hold on.
Rest,

Weary knight
You journey home.

Calhoun Hill

On Calhoun hill,
Resting among a golden field.
The sky goes on forever,
Leading to mischief endeavors.

Nature is at its best,
The white tail deer rest.
Cardinal whistles a tune,
A maple tree looms.

The mountains are a breathing taking view,
Under an ocean of blue.
Rabbits bounce and play,
An angry squirrel takes on the day.

Nature creates it's own pace,
Serenity finds a place.
Resting among a golden field,
On Calhoun Hill.

The Fiddle

The banjo plays,
The fiddle sways,
Clogging to the beat,
The sound of Blue Grass under my feet.

Voices carry through the night,
As my feet take to flight.
Clogging to the beat,
The sound of Blue Grass under my feet.

The fiddle rings loud,
Over a Saturday night crowd.
Clogging to the beat,
The sound of Blue Grass under my feet.

Memories Long Spent

It is time to back away,
We have had our time in the sun.
Time to be moving on,
I will pass by this way again someday.

Storm clouds are moving in,
Boxes are packed,
The luggage is stacked.
Back to the beginning again.

We can not have forever,
There are many bridges to burn.
Another life lesson learned,
I will forget, never.

One more moment,
The tears fall more.
Fate is knocking at my door,
I say farewell to memories long spent.

Forgiveness is for the Bold

Forgiveness is for the bold,
A constant battle,
Found within the soul.
The light of truth,
Condemned since youth.
Not forgetting,
Not forgiving.
Another sorrow is carried,
The past will never be buried.
Nothing,
A lesser thought,
A battle that must be fought.
Courage will make you whole,
Forgiveness is for the bold.

Music

When you dance with me,
Step by step,
I feel the music,
Lost within time.
Fabric whirls
Gracefulness swirls.
Around the floor,
I become lost.
A smile
A tear,
I feel you near.
Soft embrace,
As the music plays.
Content I feel,
When you dance with me.

Removing selfishness

I smell the scent of my little girls hair,
Complexion so fare.
She lets out a cry,
I let out a whimsical sigh.

She is my life,
A wonderful delight.
A desire fulfilled
The world seems still.

A tiny life,
A magical sight.
Overwhelmed emotions,
I watch my love and devotion.

Life's beauty is relentless,
Removing selfishness.
The world stands still,
As a miracle becomes real.

Winter Night

Desolate and bare,
A landscape appears.
A pale blue illumination,
Reflects under the night sky.
Wolves dance,
Calling for home.
Under a winters moon.

A howl
Lonely is the sound.
Searching,
Longing for home
Under a winters moon.

A chill
The wolves begin to cry.
Lonely is the sound,
Home is calling,
A native sound
Under a winters moon.

The Bell

The bells chime one,
Life has begun.
The bells chime two,
Exploring life's views.
The bells chime three
A soul is set free.
The bells chime four
Faith is at the door.
The bells chime five,
Struggling to survive.
The bells chime six,
Chaos is the mix.
The bells chime seven,
Ambition is driven.
The bells chime eight
Facing fate.
The bells chime nine,
Waiting for a sign.
The bells chime ten,
Loving is a sin.
The bells chime eleven,
Waiting on heaven.
The bells chime midnight,
Time to end the fight.

Yuletide Prayer

A yuletide prayer
A prayer of blessing.
Bring hope,
Bring peace.
There is many that is in need.
Bring peace
To a world that doesn't know the way.

A yuletide prayer,
A prayer of blessing
Bring joy to our hearts,
A light to those who are lost.
Forgive our mistakes,
With passionate grace.
Bring peace
To a world that doesn't know the way.

A yuletide prayer
A prayer of blessing.
Bring peace
A blessing of love may you bring,
Bring hope,
Bring peace,
To those in need,
Bring peace
To a world that doesn't know the way.

Wish of Solitude

Give me solitude
One moment .
A thought of peace,
Overwhelming schedule
Life is a race.

The heart beats faster,
Blood pressure begins to rise.
Stress takes its toll,
Solitude,
A pleasant wish.

The day move slow,
Overwhelming schedule.
Let me find my thoughts,
Slow down,
For one moment
Give me solitude.

Blair Mountain

Blair Mountain
A coal miners story is told.
Legacy's fountain,
Among the young and the old.

This is where a miners union stood tall,
A better life they believed.
A union united they would never fall,
Opportunity and hope is what they grieved.

The union stood brave and true,
They stood for workers rights.
Pride and dignity is found in a certain few,
They would not give up without a fight.

The military planes came,
Standing together they would make it through.
Blair mountain was no longer the same,
The bombs came one by one on cue.

The sky turned red,
Only a few remain.
The day the mind bled,
Hope washed away by the rain.

A memorial stands proud and strong,
Legacy's fountain.
The story can be heard in the whip-poor-wills song,
Blair Mountain.

Foreign Land of Home

Home
A foreign land.
Once a friend,
Now only a stranger.
Acceptance,
Only banishment and denial.
Animosity,
A long belated trial.
Youth,
A complicated time.
Ignorance,
A forgotten feeling.
A thought of home,
My hometown,
unfamiliar place.
Once a friend,
Now, only a stranger.
A foreign land,
Home.

Rose

She hold confidence with a crown,
As she walks through the crowd.
Rose is who she is,
She holds dignity high.

Confidence she carries,
Wearing it like a royal crown.
Stare if they must,
She won't give in.

A tear she does not shed,
A frown she does not show.
Stone is the face,
Dignity she holds.

False accusation,
The crowd roars.
Who are they to judge,
They are not judgments door.

She gracefully walks by the onlookers,
She does not care who she has crossed.
Rose is who she is,
She wears confidence with a crown.

Running

The wind is harsh upon my face,
I hear the sound of a storm.
The foot steps quicken with a steady pace,
Death is coming,
I was warned.
Running,
Running,
My own nightmare that I made,
A path with mistrust,
Mistakes made.
Afraid to look back,
I run fast.
Running,
Running,
The truth I can not tell,
My soul I will sell.
Glancing over my shoulder,
The beast quickly approaches,
I run from the same ole game.
Death is coming,
I was warned,
Running
Running
The truth I can not tell.

Untitled VIII

Whip-poor- will,
The voice is still.
Silence I hear tonight,
The dark mountains loom.

Whip-poor- will
The song is still.
Fading,
The mountains loom.

Whimsical

Whimsical
A fluttering breeze.
Refreshing
The changing of the leaves.

Autumn mist,
Drifting with lightness and ease.
Cool and crisp
A fluttering breeze.

Valance

Unraveling
A valance
Time passes
Finding balance

In the present,
Two hands will touch.
A second is spent,
A moment is rushed.

The hands of uncertainty,
The future is pushed.
Unveiling an identity,
Unraveling balance is crushed.

Lost Road

I am on a lost road,
One day I will return.
Away from the living I tread,
Mistakes I will make.
Please understand,
I have much to learn.
Chaos
I may often create,
I will soon find a way.
All I ask
Believe in me.

My life will often be a mess,
Don't lose hope.
You must have faith,
One day I will know who I am,
I will find a way.
I am on a lost road,
One day I will return,
I ask only one thing,
Believe in me.

Untitled IX

Some thing are better found,
Some things are better lost.
Some questions
Are better left unanswered.
The reason I do not know,
The reason you do not know.
Some things are better left this way,
For many reason unknown.
Some things are better found,
Some things are better lost.
A reason no one understands,
A reason many misunderstand.

Burnsville

Burnsville lake
A place I hold dear.
Friends are found,
Relaxtation is always near.

A place of memories,
Scent of honey suckle lingers in the breeze.
The water glistens,
The golden eagle gently listens.

Burnsville lake,
A place I hold dear.
A beginning,
I found here.

Love showed the way,
On a summers day.
Something I thought I had lost,
But what was restored.

Burnsville lake,
A place I hold dear.
Friends are always found,
Love is always near.

The Bewitching Hour

The bewitching hour,
The clock strikes twice.
The essence of change
Calls my name.
The clock strikes thrice,
The hour chants my name.
Fresh is the day,
Anew circle begins.
The bewitching hour rings,
The essence of change
Calmly name.
Reborn
Within a new day.
The Bewitching hour.

I watch the Fog Rise

I watch the fog rise
The world is grey and dreary.
Through the years we become wise,
You seem so weary.

Lost in a never ending rain,
I hear the baby cry,
You leave my emotions drained.
You only sigh.

I hear the rain begin to pour,
We can work this out,
There is no need to close the door,
We only seem to scream and shout.

We still have a chance,
Love is a surprise.
You look at me through a chance,
I watch the fog rise.

Heaven is the only thing I see

I hear the longing in your voice,
I have no choice.
Your presence is near,
The desire is sheer.

A gentle hand,
Skin touches the sand.
I feel you muscles flex,
Lose all context.

I look into your eyes,
Your mouth covers my cries.
I whisper your name,
I no longer feel the same.

Surrounded by your scent,
Our bodies are spent.
I feel you all around me,
Heaven is the only thing I see.

The Country Church

A country church,
The Sunday bell rings.
In the steeple the doves perch,
Amazing Grace the congregation sings.

Life begins at the wooden door,
Here the human spirit creates its own tune.
Fighting for salvation becomes an inner war,
When the soul is left in ruins.

A new world begins,
Hope is found.
In the end faith always wins,
Sorrow kneels on the ground.

Forgive your foe,
Find peace with a tainted past.
Here the human spirit is never low,
All worries are cast.

Innocents can not be destroyed,
In the steeple doves are perched.
Love fills the void,
A country church.

Item

Something was stolen
An item with no name.
Taken
Was another day.
Taken
Was my age.
Growing,
Is the remorse of the day.
Taken
Was another day.
An item with no name,
Was stolen today.

The Valley of the Sky Lark

In the valley where the sky lark nest,
A place that never rest.
Unknown grave lie,
Under a grass that is high.

The fires still burn against the night sky,
Anguish still cries.
A state of discord raised tempers,
Defeat was found with a moaning whimper.

The grass is stained crimson,
Hate is a prison.
A black bird calls,
Where thousands fall.

Indifference causes strife,
Oppression takes life.
Greed starts a war,
Revenge is evil allure.

Human tears are shed,
No end to the dead.
The light of the day grows dark,
Voices are heard in the song of the lark.

Mournful is the rain.
A culture is in wane.
The sunrise brings
Silence rings.

A land is drained,
Another war ends in vain.
Spirits do not rest,
In the valley where the sky lark nest.

"Understanding Confusion"

Understanding confusion,
A difficult task to do.
Sit back and sigh,
Ask the heavens why?
Twisting and pulling,
Time to let go,
Loneliness devours,
Past is old,
Tomorrow is for the bold.

What is pain?
What is remorse?
Twist and turn,
Two paths converge.
A reality was once a dream,
Made by a twisted decision,
Farewell is long,
Slowly fade.

Fate,
Fate is reaching within the known.
Searching for a meaning,
I only come up empty.
Twisting and pulling,
Time to let go,
Ignoring the final decision,
While I try to understand confusion

Twila Nicholas

"A Dream is Harmony"

A dream is harmony,
Time is reality.
Where has the moment gone?
One minute,
One second;
Another hour is done.
Harmony and time,
Do they really belong?
A vision is life,
Reality is the way.
A small calculation,
Continuing figuration.
Time is reality,
A dream is harmony.

Twila Nicholas
March. 18, 1997

"Toward A Place Unknown"

A long ways from home I tread;
I do not walk, nor do I run.
Gliding along toward where I am lead;
Following the burning sun.

Walking forward
From a place I once knew.
Fate leads me wayward,
Disappearing into an ocean of new.

The years of youth go by;
The road has been long.
The years fly,
Gods leads my hand to where I belong.

My mind is leery,
A destination far from home.
My soul is weary,
As I am slowly lead toward a place unknown.

"We Only Judge"

Trying to find a way,
When the road is long.
Judgment has the final say,
Even when thoughts are wrong.

Another dead end,
One more person has the final say.
Judgment is a harsh wind,
The ground is what people lay.

Keep on going,
The wrong way is right,
More people scorning,
The right way is only a fight.

Who has the right to judge?
We are all still learning,
Yet we only know how to hold a grudge,
Society is so discerning.

Twila Nicholas
June 1998

"The Meaning"

Devotion
Commitment
What is the meaning.
A sign of responsibility;
Loving devotion.
Eagerness,
Long awaited feelings;
What is the meaning.
Human emotion,
The control of the mind.
A sign of commitment;
A loving devotion.
Love,
A feeling
An emotion;
What is the meaning.

Twila Nicholas
2000

"Vanishing Silence"

The stillness before the dawn,
The heavens whisper.
The darkest hour of night,
A mystery is unveiled.

The calm before a storm,
A light shines.
Nature takes a breath,
A mystery appears.

The silence before a war,
The heavens sigh.
A dark cloud forms,
A mystery vanishes.

Twila Nicholas
2001

"Yesterdays End"

Yesterdays end,
Looming ghost;
A child's laughter,
Sings,
Yesterday song.
I walk along,
Down a shaded path;
Beneath a old oak tree,
I rest.

Magnificent and tall,
Branches still remain;
Hot summer day,
I find time to rest.
A place,
Where I will find yesterday;
My soul,
My heart
Lays beneath,
Wooden branches.

A jaded canopy,
Along a shaded path;
Childhood memories slowly fade.
A ghost,
A spirit,
Realization,
The foresight of truth;
Youth,
A path finally ends.

Down a shaded path,
Sweet sorrow;
Cherished youth.
Still, I see;
A looming ghost.
I hear,
A child's laughter,
Time is my youth;
Yesterdays end.

Twila Nicholas
April. 20, 2002

"Spiritual Death"

Change
Lays upon the hands.
Unexpected,
Unwanted,
Accepting
Is not an option.
Point of view changes,
No longer recognizing
Ideals.
Hours,
Are broken.
Time,
Has no meaning.
Unexpected,
Unwanted,
A way of life is gone.
Fading
Give a way to change.
Change,
Lays upon the hands.
Unexpected,
Unwanted,
Not believing.
Creation,
Has no meaning,
Accepting,
Is not an option,
Change,
Lay upon the hands.

Twila Nicholas

"Sorrow Is The Darkest Hour"

Abuse,
Another bruise.
Mental anguish,
Purple and blue.
A broken body,
A cry is unheard;
Sorrow is the darkest hour.

A crime.
Witness?
Chosen to be unseen;
Death over comes the soul.
None stand accused,
Everyone is to blame.

Meek voice,
Silence is deception,
A hollow grave remains.
A broken spirit,
A cry goes unheard,
Sorrow is the darkest hour.

Twila Nicholas

"Destiny's Threshold"

Standing on a threshold
Rose petals on the ground.
Life's love and devotion,
Stands at the altar.

A destiny awaits,
Watching the candle wax burn;
Flame of desire burns,
Ivey vine entwines.

Bells are ringing,
Down the aisle love stares;
The future is calling,
A solid path where tomorrow walks.

Two lives will interweave,
Expression of feelings unveiled,
Two lives will never be the same.
The tears of fate begin to fall.

Looking down an aisle of uncertainty,
Love is waiting at the altar,
Fate opens the door.
Standing on a threshold.

Twila Nicholas
2005

"Whole"

The beauty of being whole;
All cards are on the table.
The truth is finally told;
A mistake has no label.

Erase past mistakes;
A person becomes bold.
Self-conflict no longer rakes
The beauty of being whole.

Twila Nicholas

"Hate With No Reason"

Heinous act,
Speaks forbidden words,
Words of hate,
Ever to gently
Rolls from the tongue.

Freedom to speak,
Hold with dignity.
Animosity has the say;
One point of view
Taken the wrong the way.

Hate is a weakness;
Heinous act
Freely committed.
No remorse
The human spirit is dark
A person is lost.

Twila Nicholas
1998

"Autumn Leaves"

Autumn leaves float toward the ground,
Along a rocky cliff she travels,
Long black satin gown,
Chains of sadness unravels.

Loves tragedy is unveiled,
She walks alone,
Life is derailed,
Waiting for her love to journey home.

She waits for hope,
Appearing at her own free will,
She can no longer cope,
The skyline she searches still.

A soul that doesn't rest,
Silent foot steps walk upon the ground,
She still looks to the west,
As autumn leaves float toward the ground.

Twila Nicholas
July 1999

"Spirit of Past Sins"

Array of purple and white,
Light up the night sky.
Approaching storm at night,
A predator creeps nearby.

A deep voice is shallow,
Thunder rumbles,
Voices chant down the hollow,
Feel the blood of the humble.

Horrid deed is unraveled,
Vengeful spirit towers,
Yesterdays sins travel,
The wind smells sour.

Cold rain begins to pour,
Storm winds groan.
Blood stains the floor,
The remains of the unknown

Lightning flashes,
Moaning among the wind
A light flashes,
A spirit of past sins.

Twila Nicholas
2002

"Coincidence"

An obstacle;
An obstacle;
Was defeated today.
A simple task
A complicated task,
One that was succeeded.
Closing my eyes,
Taking a breath,
Leaping with faith.
Blind and confused,
An accident
Some would presume.
Ironic coincidence
A simple task
A complicated task
A leap of faith some would say.
An obstacle,
An obstacle
I defeated today.

Twila Nicholas

"Confidant and True"

Where ever you may go,
Head held high,
Confidant and true,
Gracing presence your own way.

Personality that shines,
No obstacles are denied
Just keep going,
Not caring what people say.

Inner beauty is rare,
Walk with dignity,
No cares,
Curiosity will stare.

Have no shame,
Beliefs and values,
Character is born,
A necessity to hold.

No one else will never compare,
Self-respect is a prize indeed.
Always remain confidant and true,
Where ever you may go.

Twila Nicholas
July 2003

"Heart Beat"

Smooth skin,
I watch you breath.
You begin to stir,
I worship you.

Breath in your scent,
I watch you sleep.
Touch your face,
I explore your form.

Your are my dream,
I watch you move.
Desire flames,
I hear your heart beat.

Twila Nicholas
2005

"Spring Rain"

Rain
Calling my name.
Running
Through a crystal stream.
Calling
nature beckons to me.
Vibrant and free,
Twirling
Feel the rain.
Coolness on my skin,
The spirit sings.
The rain is falling.
Calling,
The spirit follows.
Running,
Through a crystal stream.
Rain,
Calling my name.

Twila Nicholas

"Loves Last Dance"

Loves last dance,
Take a chance,
Reach out for me;
Love is all I see
I feel your sould,
The pounding of our hearts;
We will soon depart.
Hold me
One last time,
Seperation;
Cruel and unkind.
Safe and secure,
This one moment,
This night will soon be spent;
I will always love you.
True love,
Bound,
Forever in a lifetime.
Morning comes,
Dawn arrives to soon.
You touch my face,
Love has left
An eternal trace.
I feel the pounding
Of the souls heart;
I am left in a trance.
We dance,
Loves last dance.

Twila Nicholas
April 2006

"Painted Glass"

Hidden window,
Created of painted glass.
Mysterious and unknown,
The truth is found;
Secrets revealed,
Thoughts clearly read.

Illumination of painted glass;
Hidden window,
The place,
Where the depths of understanding
Are found.
The truth awaits
For those who seek it.

Understanding of creation,
Where love and hate collide.
Confusion,
Is easily seen.
Visions of imagination,
Is seen.
Mysterious and unknown,
Created of painted glass;
Hidden window.

Twila Nicholas
2006

"Tremble"

She trembles,
Frighten and alone;
Ragged and forlorn.
Her heart is torn,
Quietly, she waits.
A story her life tells,
Yet, no one cares.
A misfit,
Wanting to blend in.
Society turns a shoulder,
Giving a sly grin.
Only an outcast,
She struggles in vein;
Trying to blend in.
Tired and tattered,
She stumbles along.

A misfit,
Creating her own elegance;
Beauty is found within.
Different,
She sighs.
Society carries on.
Still,
She sits,
Frighten and alone;
Ragged and forlorn.
She struggles,
Trying to blend in.

One lonely soul,
A long story to tell;
She stumbles along.
Society,
Cruel and cold.
No one looks,
No one cares,
Frighten and alone;
Ragged and forlorn.
She waits,
She trembles.

Twila Nicholas
June 2007

"Scarlet Sky"

A scarlet sky,
Bridges burning,
A muffled cry,
Hatred is churning.

Never ends,
Humans have many sins,
The wound hatred deepens,
No one wins.

Hurtful ambition,
A day of dread,
Consumed by a negative vision,
A soul becomes dead.

The future is only the past,
The morning is high,
Hatred is cast,
Under a scarlet sky.

Twila Nicholas
April. 18, 2002

"Bound"

I feel ill,
I could be better.
A humans free will
Burned letters.

This is not my mess,
I am not the one to blame.
I am estimated for being less,
Traveling a one way lane.

A simple cure.
I am an eye sore.
What just happened is a blur,
The same way is a bore.

Never come back,
I won't be around.
Trying to figure out what I lack,
I am no where bound.

Twila Nicholas
2000

"The Unknown"

In a unknown place
Suffering shadows the day.
An unclear realm,
Coldness consumes.
A broken promise,
Creates a forbidden place.
Grief
Leads the way,
Crushes the soul.

A world created,
From heart ache and pain.
Suffering,
Anguish,
Greed takes a breath.
Coldness consumes,
Souls find no rest,
A land of plentiful,
Turns to dust.

A gentle whisper
A prayer
For peace,
Justification.
A dream of home,
A promise that was never shown.
A sorrowful plead.
The spirit is left in ruins.

A better day,
Change,
Hope shadows the day.
A broken promise,

The word of decree.
Peace of tomorrow,
A place,
Where remorse is shown.
Unknown realm,
Anguish,
An unknown place.

Twila Nicholas
1999

"Cringe"

You make me cringe,
Our beliefs differ,
The tension is high,
Your voice keeps screaming.

Politics and religion,
Destroy a good feeling,
One more complaint,
The roof is crashing in.

You only argue about everything,
Think you know best,
Point of view taken,
You arouse my agitation.

Fact or fiction?
I don't care,
My mind only aches,
You make me cringe.

Twila Nicholas
2004

"Secret Turmoil"

Only silence;
When I should hear noise,
Only sadness;
When I should be laughing.
The clouds are dark;
The wind is bitter;
I am lost in a world of chaos;
Only destruction
Do you listen;
Do you care?
Hidden turmoil within my mind
I am dieing within,
You don't understand.
Commotion surrounds me,
Life is crashing down,
I slip away,
A lost voice in the darkness;
Never to be found.
I am silent
Consume by despair
Lost is my soul
I am screaming within,
You don't understand.

Twila Nicholas
April 10, 2007

"Time to Rest"

Ancient sugar maple,
Whisper softly,
Branches twist and turn,
Age lithely with time.

Red leaves,
Float upon the crisp autumn wind,
Generation to generation,
Sway in harmony.

A voice grows old,
Limbs grow empty,
Time to rest,
Ancient sugar maple.

Twila Nicholas
November 2006

"Shades"

Sweet scent
The scent
Of the spring rain.
Sweet scent
The scent
Of lilacs in bloom.

Sweet sight,
The sight
Of daffodils in the sun.
Sweet sight,
The sight
Of a new sunrise.

Twila Nicholas

"Solid Gold"

The color blue,
Wedding vows ring true,
A soft touch,
Love is not rushed.

Hope is a new
While doves rest in the mews,
A new era begins,
Life without sin.

Family morals are used,
Two lives become musedj
Bells ring,
Faith is found on a doves wings.

Advice is borrowed
Encouraging a new tomorrow.
Solid gold.
Love is a mystery to behold.

Twila Nicholas

"Taught"

Where kindness is taught,
Memories can't be bought.
An isolated place,
The modern world leaves no trace.

A quiet town,
Where sorrows drown.
A friendly smile,
Makes a day worth while.

Home cooked meal at the diner,
Proud to be a coal miner.
Every noon the church bell rings,
The blue grass sings.

Laughter is always heard,
Hospitality well served.
Happiness is never sought,
Where kindness is taught.

Twila Nicholas
June. 9, 2004

"Green"

I know a place,
Where sorrow is erased.
Don't need to go,
I already know.

Gossip,
Notorious for being hip.
No place for the bashful,
A person will get an ear full.

Drunks stumble around,
Waiting for one to hit the ground.
A marital affair is seen,
In the public eye everything is keen.

Slurred speech,
Modesty is breeched.
Gossip galore,
A roar travels out the door.
Smoke filled room,
Loud voices loom.
Glasses ring,
Karoke is the thing.

Drunk up the tab,
Call a cab,
I haven't been seen,
Turning green.

Twila Nicholas
2003

"The ambition of Passion"

A dim glow
Lights
The night sky.
Yearning,
Consumed
By inner desire.
Reckless thoughts,
The ambition of passion
Slowly burns.

Flames
Burn recklessly.
One lesson
The soul never learns
Self control
When emotions beckon.
Condemn becomes the soul;
When,
The ambition of passion
Slowly burns.

Twila Nicholas

"The Death of Desire"

A spring breeze
Calls for me.
Ebon rose
Petals shed.
Free
I want to be;
Petals tumble toward the ground.

Spring breeze
Death is calling for me.
Unshed tears
Petals shed;
Trapped
By the anguish of desire.
Free
I want to be;
Petals tumble toward the ground.

A spring breeze
Calls for me.
Ebon rose
The petals shed.
Hope I believe,
I will never see.
Free
I want to be
Petals tumble toward the ground.

Twila Nicholas
1998

"Tonight"

Thoughts of home;
Thoughts of love.
The mind strays tonight;
Toward a place long ago.
Past moves on
The future is given.
A life once lived;
Exist no more.

Childhood,
A day
When everything was blesses;
Time had not been set.
Cherish the day
Eating sweets.
Dreaming of tomorrow;
Opportunities were strong.

The innocent wish
Upon many things.
Dreaming of tomorrow,
When tomorrow still had wings.
The mind strays tonight
Toward a place long ago.
Thoughts of love,
Thoughts of home.

Twila Nicholas

"Cold Sun"

In a world of nightmares,
I search for blue skies.
Brown grass below me,
It is difficult to walk with grace.

Confused,
So much chaos;
Betrayed by a friend,
Reality becomes a nightmare.

Heart ache and disappointment is death,
When a friendship ends.
A open door forever remains shut,
No trust can be found in the world.

I see no sun,
Only coldness;
Fate is bitter,
When I am betrayed by a friend.

Twila Nicholas
1996

"Love Is"

Love is a soft smile of a newborn baby;
First kiss in the summer rain.
Finding hope for a fatal illness;
Security found in a mothers embrace.
Love is a heartfelt farewell;
Soft wind of a butterfly wing,
A fathers protection;
Gentle wool of a lamb.
Love is the faith of the living;
Secret shared between friends.
Lilacs in spring,
Holiday cheer;
Love is the soft embrace of an intimate lover.
Affection from a loyal pet,
Hope, forgiveness, and kindness;
Love is the creation of the world.

Twila Nicholas
1995

"Self-Hate"

Angry and frustrated,
Only disappointed,
Freely agitated,
Wanting to be respected.

You slowly turn hard hearted.
When did the violence start?
Kindness has departed,
Life is no longer a work of art.

Life leaves you in doubt,
A hard lonely road you choose to follow,
Frustration shows the wrong route,
A road of disappointment you become hollow.

Lost by aggravation,
Rage consumes you,
Self-respect hangs in levitation,
A dangerous life is what you brew.

Turning your back on life,
Forgiveness is no where found,
Hard heartedness only causes strife,
Anger is a tragic path toward the cold ground.

Twila Nicholas
September. 14, 2001

"Solid Reflection"

A strange is what I see,
Torment grips the heart,
The mind is no longer free,
Inner battle tares the soul apart.

Locked away
Depression is a souls grave,
Life begins to sway,
There is nothing left to save.

Drifting alone,
Sanity is gone,
No where is home,
Dark is the dawn.

A reflection,
How could this be?
Poisonous mental infection,
A stranger is what I see.

Twila Nicholas
2000

"Human Wings"

Heaven shines down
Hope is restored.
Inner strength is found
Endurance endeavors.
The will to fight,
Not to give in.
Fate is listening,
Heaven shines down.
Keep fighting
Strength will come.
Hope is restored
Courage will carry on.
Death is not yet knocking
Knocking at life's door.
Believe
Believing that you will survive
Once more.

Keep fighting,
Self-defeat,
Is a constant allure,
Hope is restored,
Finding courage
Within the will to live.
The battle is constant,
Pray
Endurance will be given.
The will to fight,
Unseen war.
Fate is listening,
Human wings
Will eventually sore.

Twila Nicholas

"Hidden"

There is you,
There is me,
So close,
Yet we do not touch.
Contentment,
Once existed,
Wondering through the years,
Love is slowly spent.

Drifting,
Drifting apart.
Knowing each others thoughts,
Now,
Two minds apart.
Words,
Go unspoken,
Communication is broken.

We are one
Now time has begun.
One soul,
Divides,
Never again will feel whole.
So close,
Yet we do not tough.
Difference pass,
Love is slowly spent.
There is you,
There is me.

Twila Nicholas

"Wicked Smile"

Wicked smile,
Tongue lashes of vile.
Seeks it prey,
Leads in dismay.

Not knowing what it wants,
It only taunts.
Sinister is the prison,
Only takes, nothing is given.

Freely it roams,
Settling, close to home.
A manipulative style,
Wicked smile.

Twila Nicholas

"The Sign of Divine"

Looking for a sign;
Love is divine.
Waiting for me;
Drifting on a never ending sea.

Looking for a sign;
Hope so divine.
Patiently I wait;
Yearning for heavens gates.

Looking for a sign;
Life so divine.
Waiting for a second tomorrow;
Carried on the wings of a sparrow.

Looking for a sign;
Love is so divine.
Waiting for me;
The depths of the soul I shall see.

Twila Nicholas
April 2002

"The Wound is Deep"

The wound is deep,
Feel the blood seep.
The world burns,
No one seems to learn.

Death and damnation carried,
Sorrow yearns to be buried.
The world has turned cold,
Anger is in the eyes of the bold.

Glory, revenge, and triumph,
Greed makes the heart pump.
Searching for a revelation,
Finding no destination.

Animosity leads the way,
Destruction has the final say.
Feel the blood seep,
The wound is deep.

Twila Nicholas
September 2002

"Appealing"

Everything becomes appealing,
I stare at the ceiling.
The is keen,
Future yet to be seen.

Perfect sense,
Life can be intense.
Progress is slowly made,
Troubled waters are some times wade.

In time everything will pass,
All possibility comes in great mass.
Living life is a great feeling,
Everything becomes appealing.

Twila Nicholas

"Time to let Go"

Life is a struggle,
Separated from dreams;
Personal world is crashing down.
Deception until the very end;
Yearning for a promotion.
Discovering something better;
Youth doesn't last forever.
Yearning for peace within the mind;
Not wanting to let go,
Solving the puzzle to life's meaning.
Lessons learn,
Tomorrow is a new dawn;
Now is the time to let go.

Twila Nicholas
June 1996

"Waiting for You"

Morbid day,
Mirage of the past,
You are no longer near;
I walk a lonely path.

A picture of you flashes before me,
I feel your spirit follow me.
Today becomes yesterday;
Your vision is all I see.

The dream is clear;
I see you sitting by the old covered bridge.
This is where you always waited for me,
Love is all I see.

Engulfed in the morning mist;
A fishing pole you hold,
Sun begins to rise,
You take my hand.

We walk along the river bank;
Cat tails flutter in the breeze.
The world stops;
Your arms wrap around me.

Pure is the first kiss;
Love is the essence of time.
The water cascades;
Your warmth surrounds me.

The present unfolds;
Your memory fades.
Morning dew begins to fall;
Cry out you name.

Stumble through a row a graves;
Your name is clear,
Single red rose,
I kneel on the ground.

Each day you fade further away;
Lay next to you,
Wishing for my last breath,
Waiting for your loving hand

"Aware"

You watch me,
I glance.
Curious,
The mind is indecision.
Deception,
Infatuation,
Maybe,
Love,
You watch me.
Like a predator,
Contemplating it's prey.

You watch me,
Inquisitive glance;
Seductive look.
The soul consumes,
Mysterious stare,
Hate,
Disgust,
Maybe;
Regret.
I am aware,
You watch me.

"Bad"

Bad,
Is the feeling.
Horror,
Is the emotion.
Caught,
Is the crisis.
Explaining,
Is the problem.
Why,
Ones does not know.
Reason,
Beyond the understanding.
Caught,
Is the situation.
Horror,
Is the impulse.
Bad,
Is the feeling.

"Wounded"

Lifeless eyes,
Drifting in a dream
The spirit falls
Screaming a cry.
Wounded is the day
When a spirit falls.
Grieving,
A finished dawn.
Wounded is the day
When a spirit falls.
Oppression
Condemns all.
Screaming a cry
Lifeless eyes.

Untitled X

My solitude;
A world of
Crimson and blue.
Dreaming
Believing.
Living,
An illusion.
Drifting,
Endless stream
Of dreams.
Seeing,
Crimson and blue,
My solitude.

Untitled XI

Who knows where life really began,
How did god really create the land?
Sturdy and strong it will always stand.
The land will and god knows it can.

There is a spirit here, can't you see;
Animals are wild and birds are free.
The trees are always green,
There is soul that will never leave.

When evil is upon the land,
Life is not so grand,
God will not let it stand,
Grace is gods hand.

Generations will come and go,
The wind will always blow;
The land will always flourish and grow,
Nature always puts on a show.

When all works are said at the end of the day,
Fighting is at bay;
People have a debt to pay;
Nature will find a way to stay.

Twila Nicholas
August 1994

Untitled XII

Covered by the shade
The oak tree sways.
The is accurately made,
As a breeze floats my way.

Dreams become slow,
Losing track of time.
Drifting lithely upon a meadow,
I find a peace of mind.

My place to be discovered,
Let time be lost.
A secret veil is uncovered,
Nature has no cost.

Twila Nicholas

Untitled XIII

Step away from me,
I am not your toy.
These games grow old,
I am raging.

Aggravation is the word,
There is no trust,
Communication is lost,
No respect.

What is in your head?
Neither one of us understands,
Lost is the situation,
No more you or me.

No reason to try,
Unfaithfulness is all you know.
I have no kind feelings,
Step away from me.

Untitled IV

My reflection
I can no longer see.
The image is cloudy
The person,
Unrecognizable.
My reflection,
Despair I see,
Self-pity consumes me.
The twilight hour approaches,
A silent wound still bleeds deep.
My reflection,
Transparent,
From a sudden transfiguration.
Secrets deepen,
The silence is held,
As the night darkens.
My reflection,
I can no longer know.
Despair consumes the youth,
Secrets of a transfiguration.
Healing
A silent wound;
Found from within
My own reflection.

"Keen"

Trapped by my own thoughts,
An inner scream;
Turmoil of pain.
Cry mercy,
Gods face appears;
A sign,
My soul is forever lost.

Love is forgotten;
Demolish trust.
The soul is rotten,
I feel life
Turning to dust.

A chance,
A never ending nightmare;
A demons dance.
A leap of trust,
My own anguish I create,
Naïve;
Horrid mistake;
It was mine to take.

"Humiliation"

My eyes deceive me,
Disbelief is what I see.
Fighting to be bold,
As my soul turns cold.

I walk by the sea,
Discovering that no longer are we.
Fate holds us in it arms,
Life has sinister charms.

I hold my tongue,
How foolish the young.
Tension is all around,
My humiliation is scattered among the ground.

Endless is heartache,
In a devastating world the greedy take.
A love affair didn't show,
My frustration grows

Another story ends,
The rancor deepens.
Crash a blissful day,
Humiliation walks away.

Twila Nicholas
June 24, 1998

"Betrayals Web"

Mixed emotions,
Lost devotion;
Caught in a rage,
I feel the soul begin to rage.

Innocents in shreds,
Tomorrow is another day I dread;
Freedom of the soul is far,
Humiliation leaves a scar.

I want to leave,
Regrets I grieve;
The truth comes to late,
Memories become a weight.

Betrayal screams,
Closer is difficult to redeem;
Peoples voices chatter,
One day this moment will not matter.

My only cure,
Shut deceits door.
Healing I must try.
Forgetting the lies.

I am misplaced,
Rumors time will erase.
A constant spider web,
Where betrayal had led.

Twila Nicholas
1997

"The Day is at it's Peak"

A winter ocean,
Changing season
I feel love
Rays cascade from above.
Illusion;
Spring mist,
I feel the wind wisp.

Feelings of the soul are undone,
A new beginning has come.
A soft tear falls from the eyes.
I watch the seagulls fly.
We have a new fight,
The day started so bright.
We seem to live many different lives,
To many personalities in one hive.

Life brings many things,
Even a new meaning.
The seagulls coast on the breeze,
The ocean waves breath.
Freedom is so sweet,
The is at its peak.

Twila Nicholas
April 12, 2002

"Shine"

In the dim candle light,
A mind wonders,
A dark night,
Reflections of the past ponders.

What went wrong,
Reflection in the mirror,
Remembering a song,
A reflection never seem more clearer.

Pounding heart beat,
Feel the sweat,
This is not self-defeat,
Justice will be met.

The walls grow dark,
Listening for a sound,
Unknown feelings I embark,
Life's simple deceptions hound.

A reflection shines,
An inner sight,
Infidelity grinds,
In the dim candle light.

"Found"

Disoriented season,
Events happen without a reason.
Leaves fall,
Waiting for the thaw.

No one has complete control,
A complete circle is made whole.
Search for closer within,
Grievance will find no end.

Nature has a way,
Renovating a day.
Emptiness is found,
A humble cry makes a sound.

Twila Nicholas
2005

"A Moment Lost"

A moment is lost,
Squandering in self-pity.
Absent from life,
Anguish is strife.
Past mistakes,
Done and made.
Looking back,
The future is blocked.
Take care of now,
Forget the mistakes;
Learning is living.
Fretting
Waist to much space.
Worrying
A moment is lost.

Twila Nicholas

"The House Burns Bright"

The house burns bright,
Agitation is the light.
You didn't come home.
I was left all alone.

Aggression follows me,
You are the only picture I see.
Delusional,
Everything is unusual.

You are no where to be seen,
Emotions are keen,
Apprehension is high tonight,
The house burns bright.

Twila Nicholas

"Seducing Passion"

Sensuality,
Hidden divinity.
Human refrain,
Sensual sanctions.
Shameful?
Human is human,
Pleasure is a feeling.
Sensuality,
Seducing passion;
Self control has no restraints,
Sensuality is discovered.
The mind,
The body,
Completely tossed,
Purity is forever lost.

Twila Nicholas
March. 21, 2006

"Restlessness"

I fantasize about green eyes,
A chill in the night air,
Lightning cascades across the sky,
A presence is near.

Eerie sound of an owl,
Crickets chant,
A coyote howls,
A dark night rants.

Scent of fresh cut hay,
Leaves rustle,
Scared rabbit runs away,
A shadow hustles.

Footsteps on the porch floor,
Restlessness turns to fear,
A knock at the door,
Green eyes appear.

Twila Nicholas
2002

"Justification"

Searching for closure,
Through justification.
Frustration
Everything becomes a tangled mess.
Tears of remorse;
A mistake made.
The greave has been dug,
A life fades.
Memories cherished
A deed,
A wrongful act.

Grasping for hope,
Struggling for faith.
Frustration looms
Anguish,
Sorrow fills the soul.
Retaliation,
Searching for closure,
Through justification.

Twila Nicholas

"Mountain Breeze"

A cool mountain breeze;
On summers eve.
The day breathes it's last,
As the sun begins to pass.

A solid farewell
Essence of time dwells.
Creation finds a meaning
Life is always weaning.

Hear a whisper within the sunset,
The day finds rest.
Colors of vibrant light,
Consumes the sight.

Time is at an end,
Within the evening wind.
Gentle is the summers eve,
Cool is the mountain breeze.

Twila Nicholas

"Unknown Grave"

Unknown grave,
Located near a cave.
Fearful sound,
A concealed secret waiting to be found.

A valley where the highest mountains peeks,
Waiting for peace a spirit seeks.
Yearning for rest,
An endless quest.

Forgotten story,
One that is frightful and gory.
Stagnant scents lingers in the fog,
A shallow grave lay under a splintered log.

A lost soul tries to speak,
The trees sway and creek.
Death will always rave,
Unknown grave.

Twila Nicholas
2002

"Memories by the River"

Down by the river,
The train whistles,
We swim along the waters edge,
Bath in the sun.

Relax under the willow tree,
Watch the turtles glisten in the sun
Drift asleep to the sound of trout splashing
Down by the river all day long

Live on the waters edge,
Camp all night
Excitement and laughter,
Catfish until dawn.

Worship the day,
Coal barges slither by,
Music carries in the wind,
The will soon be spent.

Love and friends,
Memories create;
Life is sedate,
Down by the river.

Twila Nicholas

"The Silence"

Silence
A horrifying sound.
Silence
The loneliest of thought.
Silence
The lost words of conversation.
Silence
The bitter feeling of insecurity.
Silence
The wail of despair.
Silence
The rage of anger.
Silence
The bitter feeling of rejection.
Silence
The tragic event of misfortune.
Silence
The mourning of death.
Silence
The bitter feeling of shock.
Silence
The hidden emotion of the soul.
Silence
A horrifying sound.

Twila Nicholas
June 2003

"Temptation"

I hear a calling,
Calling out my name,
Temptation is what I see,
I deny in vane.
Sensual and sinister,
Destruction comes in many ways.
Disturbing,
I hear it calling.
I go,
I am followed.
Like a seed
Searching for a place to sow.
A fantasy,
An illusion.
I deny in vane, temptation begins to scream.
Try to pray,
It tries to prevail.
I slowly turn away,
Temptation,
Turns my way

Twila Nicholas
2003

"Only Human"

Only human
Some say
Is the greatest gift.
Others will say
Is the greatest curse.
Who is right?
Who is wrong?
The beauty,
Of being
Only human.

Creation
The greatest life.
Feeling
Emotions
Rare gift.
Different points of views
Give color
To a bland universe.
The beauty
Of being
Only human.

Mistakes
We are aloud to make.
Learning
Is human.
Choices
Integrity
Finding ones character.
Exploring

Becoming different
A unique personality.
The beauty
Of being
Only human.

Does fate
Follow life?
Maybe
Life follows fate.
What is the true depths
Of existing.
God
Evolution
Imagining
What is the meaning
Not knowing
Sometimes
Is the better way.
The beauty
Of being
Only human.

Twila Nicholas

"Thin"

Observe the minutes of the clock,
Hear the tick and tock.
Second by second,
Time beckons.

The hour hand drifts,
Yet, moves swift.
The minutes wined in sequence,
Another hour is hence.

Seconds turn in hours,
A thin hand has all the power.
Time can only mock,
The minutes of the clock.

Twila Nicholas'
1997

"Orange Light"

The middle of nowhere,
Wonder if it exist,
I watch people stare,
Make a face, can't resist.

A big crowd,
So much noise,
Voices are loud,
I try to find poise.

The air is thick,
Pollution is high,
I feel social anxiety kick,
Calm is what I try.

Restlessness,
A place that never sleeps,
Peacefulness,
Insomnia seeps.

Orange street light,
In a place without a care,
Metal structures are the only sight,
The middle of nowhere.

Twila Nicholas
September 6, 1998

"Evergreen"

Deep evergreen forest,
A soulful chorus.
Silence all around,
Pine cones lay on the ground.

Pine limbs whisper,
The air is crisper.
Lazy shade,
Foliage doesn't fade.

I breath the scent of pine,
A simple place to unwind.
Under the green canopy I wait,
Not caring if time is late.

Twila Nicholas
October 1998

"Hopeful Prayer"

One final prayer,
She whispers.
Believing in her faith,
Teary eyed;
She begins to pray.
Hoping beyond hope,
A miracle is on the way.

With inner strength,
Faith is anew.
She prays,
Life's lessons;
Learning the way.
Trial and tribulation,
Life becomes a mess;
A soul strays.

Lost,
Redemption is found.
A soul to find,
She only prays,
That soon;
Hope will show the way.

She kneels,
Believing in her faith.
A dark light will soon fade;
She whispers,
One final prayer.

"Fortress"

Near a forest edge,
A thoroughbred stands.
A long a cliffs ledge,
Causeway is found.
Along a jagged brick road,
A crumbling structure;
Ruins and decay.

Richness and power,
Stood once
In a long ancient day.
Stories imagined,
Past untold;
Once a fortress,
Now stands alone.

Dreams were made,
Laughter and excitement;
Futures path was laid.
Golden banquet hall,
Stain glass windows.
Tapestries stories
Smothered the walls;
Peace was the day,
Tranquil was the moment,

A sunless day,
Treachery showed.
A friend,
A foe was on the way.
Cloud of dust,
Fires raged,

Under siege.
Defeat burns.

Agony,
Loud screams;
Cries are still heard.
Enemy proud,
Blood stains the land.
Destruction is the path,
A broken causeway,
A ruin dream.

Desert ruins
Speak for themselves
Tragedy,
Doom.
A broken structure,
Crumbling and decay;
Souls still heard.
Spirit lingers,
On a sunless day.

Lost story
A way of life untold.
Crumbling and decay,
A fortress once stood,
Now ruins;
Where a thoroughbred stands
Near a forest edge.

Twila Nicholas
May. 25, 1999

"Tribulation"

A forgotten will,
Surviving difficulties.
Searching,
Trial and tribulation
Only follow.
Understanding,
The meaning
Of surviving difficulties.
Finding,
Life's wisdom.
Learning
Trial and tribulation.
Discovering
Difficulties have meaning.

"Slow Down"

Slow down, you travel to fast;
Life doesn't stand still,
Running from the past,
You fight against your will.

Take your time,
Moving so fast you can barely see,
Let life unwind,
Relax and let the moment be.

Slow down, you travel to fast;
Life will happen unexpectedly,
Opportunity and chance is vast,
Time already travels to fast.

Twila Nicholas
2007

"Wayward Eyes"

Inhale,
A breath,
Head held high,
One last stand.

Condemn is doubt,
A stranger frowns;
A smile,
Confidence found within.

Have faith,
Rest in the arms of fate;
Hope and courage intertwine,
One last stand.

The odds are high,
Auro of valor;
A body carries on,
Pride and dignity is found.

Exhale,
A breath,
Eyes look wayward;
One last stand.

Twila Nicholas
October 15, 2004

"The Edge of a Field"

On the edge of a field,
Where two fences meet,
You will find a small dirt hill,
Creatures with six tiny feet.

They carry ten times their body weight,
Love sunflower seeds;
Watch them crawl under a metal gate,
Scatter through the weeds.

Near the days end they begin to play,
Work hard to harvest the winter food.
Up again to meet the day,
Many predators they try to woo.

They work together,
Carry food up the small hill;
Through the worse of weather.
On the edge of a field.

Twila Nicholas
August.29, 2004

"Lavender Rose"

A lavender rose fades away,
Morbid is the day,
One last kiss,
The only wish.

Illusions in the mist,
Just one name on a very long list,
The ground begins to fall,
Heaven calls.

Spray of roses on the alter,
Emotions falter,
Visions only sway,
A lavender rose fades away.

Twila Nicholas

"My Own"

I felt sadness today.
Not of my own;
Nor,
Anyone I know.
A stranger,
I see;
A victim of a faltering regime.

A stranger with woes;
Woes I did not understand.
Lost was pride,
Dignity in shreds.
A strangers sorrow;
Became my own.

I felt remorse today.
Not of my own;
Nor,
Anyone I know.
A stranger,
I see;
A victim of a faltering regime.

Twila Nicholas

"Innocent Scream"

Innocent scream,
Roaring fire,
Tears become a stream,
Raging desire.

Judgment is one of many sins,
In the end,
No one wins,
Turmoil within the wind.

Pulse quickens,
Orange, red, and yellow;
Ambition driven,
Vanity is hollow.

Innocent victim,
Scream of mercy,
Heart beat is a steady rhythm,
Life's final curtsy.

Ashes spread all around,
Blood in the stream,
An image shatters the ground,
Innocent scream.

Twila Nicholas
September 21, 1999

"Darkness Is Unseen"

In a place unknown,
In a standard mode;
Actions no one can condone,
Somewhere on a dark road.

The ending is clear,
Reckless and abandon;
Hope only sneers,
Chances of opportunity is random.

One more dark soul,
Searching for the way home;
Innocence is stolen,
In a world where only inner demons roam.

The lost only loom,
A self-pity is darkness,
A place where love is doomed;
Nothing more, nothing less.

A darkness that is unseen,
A place where no soul should ever go;
Faith is hard to redeem,
A destination where only evil grows.

Twila Nicholas
April 1999

"Dusty Dawn"

A dusty dawn
Brings a misty haze.
Squint my eyes,
Begin to glimpse;
Across the ocean
Paradise I see.
Change is coming;
A new beginning.
Tomorrow
Is waiting for me.
Coastline forever winding
A journey begins;
Ambition pulls me.
A new direction
A better life
On tomorrows wings.
I glimpse
Across the ocean.
A new beginning
Waits for me,
Within the dusty dawn.

Twila Nicholas

"My Own Maze"

Lost in my own darkness;
Waiting for the sunshine today.
Lost in my own maze,
I alone, can create.
Stuck with a transfixed gaze,
Waiting in the shadows;
Finding a way,
Searching for realities gate.

A frown
Unknown soul,
Lonely is the heart.
Memories burn a hole,
Watching the future slowly depart.
A nightmare,
Always waiting to condole.

An illusion,
One that I have made.
Waiting for the sun shine today,
Lost in my own maze.
I am alone,
Staggering through a stagnant haze.
Waiting in the shadows,
Finding a way;
Searching for realities gate.

Twila Nicholas
November. 5, 1998

"A Decision"

I can think for myself,
Capable of choosing,
I feel like an ornament on a shelf,
Not afraid of losing.

Let me think,
Contemplation becomes alluring,
Thoughts begin to blink,
Brain waves are churning.

I can make a decision,
The outcome could be frightening,
Everything starts with a vision,
A decision could even be enlightening.

Twila Nicholas
October 2001

"Hypnotizing"

I watch a spirit fly,
Before my eyes;
Waiting on Sunday morn,
I am reborn.

Night sky,
Heaven is so high;
The earth breaths,
Resting within a night breeze.

I listen well,
The chiming of the night bell;
I feel my spirit climb,
Following an immortal vine.

Night sky,
Under the heavens I lye;
Within my sights,
Immortal imagination takes flight.

Universe constant motion,
Hypnotizing the souls inner devotion.
Before my eyes,
I watch as a spirit flies.

Twila Nicholas
December. 21, 1998

"Creation is the Dreamer"

High above the earth,
Hidden among the wind.
A soul flies in to the horizon;
The soul of a dreamer.

Love is fairytale,
Reality is backwards.
Society is no longer in focus;
The mind of a dreamer.

Society ridicules them,
Searching for what they seek.
A world of possibilities;
The eyes of a dreamer.

Colors created, life is a dance;
Human spirit is a song.
A world of innocents;
The body of a dreamer.

Creation is the dreamer,
Dull is exciting.
Hope, faith, and love;
The dream of a dreamer.

Twila Nicholas
May 1997

"Amused"

A cold winters night,
When you left my sight.
Snow was falling you walked away;
I remember as if it were yesterday.
A bar over your soul,
Dark secrets left a hole.
Passion is torture,
Knowing a secret is fortune.
Hurt and confused,
I was never amused.
Around again,
Bitter is the cold winter wind.
Wrapped in inner pain,
I don't like this game.
My own enemy,
Hosted by strange company.
Cold bitter wind bites the soul;
Please, just go.
You are hurt and confused;
Now, who is the one amused.

Twila Nicholas
1998

"The Mist"

In the twilight before dawn,
A white horse appears on the horizon,
Galloping through the mist,
Enchantment streams.

Lavender adorns its mane,
Wild and free,
Mysteriously wills,
A noble creature.

An eerie neigh,
A chill,
From nowhere
It appears.

A loud heart beat,
Rumbling of hooves,
I am complaisant,
As it gallops toward me.

Lost in the mist,
See the white of its eyes,
A vision becomes blurry,
I wake in exasperation.

Twila Nicholas
1999

"Adoration"

Adoration
Wanting
But
Not having

Finding pleasure
Yet
Not feeling
Adoring
But
Not understanding

Having the advantage
Yet
Not taking
Understanding
But
Not adoring

Feeling
Yet
Finding no pleasure
Having
But
Not wanting
Adoration.

Twila Nicholas
May 1998

"Grasping"

Distant dream
Shattered thoughts;
Hoping and yearning.
I yearn for wings,
Shattered vision.
Broken tears,
Recollection;
Over and over throughout the years.
Memoirs scour,
Again and again;
Yearning,
Learning,
An isolated destiny.
I yearn for wings,
Only to fly.
No more questions of why;
Answers have no meaning.
Thoughts isolated,
I create my own haze.
Grasping sanity,
Constant race;
The mind is a ruinous place.

Twila Nicholas
May. 20, 1998

"Forbidden Desire"

Mortality has no chance,
Deception ignites a fire,
A second glance
Threshold of naked desire.

Skin to skin,
Tow worlds come crashing down.
Heartbreak comes in the end,
A scandal is bound.

Desire begins to flame,
Tragedy on the holy alter,
Lovers with no shame,
Only ties a halter.

Passion burns,
Lust brings death,
Betrayal churns,
When passion takes a breath.

Forbidden love affair,
Emotions enhance,
Anguish begins to flare,
Mortality has no chance.

Twila Nicholas
July 18, 2002

"Blink"

A chuckle makes a sound,
Blue eyes look down,
A broken reflection staring back me,
Caring not for what I see.

A soft cry makes a sound,
Dazed look slowly comes around.
Forgotten is what I feel,
An older reflection doesn't look real.

A whimper makes a sound,
A reflection creates a frown.
To late to think,
A reflection blinks.

Twila Nicholas
November 2006

"Self-Betrayal"

A secret,
Remains hidden.
Created,
By self-betrayal.
Ticking,
Self-destruction looms.

A secret,
Remains hidden.
Desire to tell,
A flame burning;
Igniting,
Self-betrayal.

A secret,
Remains hidden.
Ticking,
Self-devastation.
Absorbing,
A desire;
A desire to tell.
Smoldering,
Creating;
Self-betrayal.

"Indifference"

Heaven cries today,
Hatred screams its name.
A small indifference,
Inner battle;
Unseen war.

Chaos leads the way,
Blood stains on the land.
Enmity wonders,
A forgotten liberty.
A small indifference,
No one seems to care;
Under a divided nation.
Screams are unheard,
Suffering is raw.
Divided by animosity,
Democracy shudders;
No one listens.
Pride is shredded;
Sorrow is the leader of the day.

Nation of citizens forgotten,
Everyone feels the pain;
When enmity wonders in vein,
Democracy is wounded,
A small indifference;
When hatred screams its name,
Heaven cries today.

Far From Grace

Far from grace,
She treads
Once a beauty with grace,
Kindness in the soul.
Bitterness and hate,
Takes its place.
Broken beauty queen,
Disappointment you endure.
Love you no longer believe,
Bitterness your life now leads.
When did you stop believing.
When did you stop feeling?
She no longer cares,
As she walks the streets of disgrace.
Once a smile covered her days,
Only a frown covers her face.
Her cries can be heard in the night air,
When did you stop believing?
When did you find despair?
A crown she was once wore,
She once walked with grace,
She no longer cares for such things.
Reborn from disappointment,
She was no longer the same.
Bitterness is found,
Kindness she no longer feels.
Broken is her dignity.
Humiliation takes its place.
She treads
Far from grace.

The Second Hand

One, two,
I count the seconds.
I hear the ticking of the hand.
One, two,
The seconds pass,
I hear the ticking of the second hand.
I feel life flowing through the veins,
Pumping, pumping;
Endlessly flowing,
One, two,
I count the seconds,
I hear the ticking of the second hand,
I listen to the life flowing through the veins.
One, two
I count the second hand.

I Believe

A fools journey,
The skeptics say
They laugh.
Writing is not for me.
A gift I believe,
They laugh at me.
This is my dream,
I believe,
Is for me.
A fool,
Skeptics say,
A dream
I will never full fill any day.
I believe
I know I will.
Set backs I find,
Accomplishment is still mine.
Skeptics laugh,
I failure I am ,
As the skeptic walks away.
A fools journey,
Some may believe,
A dream,
To me.

Vanquish

Vanquish me
Disturbed by thought.
The laughter,
The snickers,
The stares,
The wickedness still taunts.
The right to be critic,
The judgment bestowed.
In a small town,
A persons fault,
Become my own.
Human I am,
Human are you.
Laugh if you may,
Stare if you please,
I will be better,
Better than you one day.
The laughter,
The snickers,
The wickedness still taunts.
Disturbed by thought,
Accomplishment sought.
I will not quit,
My mind sets me free,
Vanquish me.

The End

Time stands still,
Tribulation test the will.
A promise betrayed,
Deception strayed.

The hands of fate,
Test the faith.
The day grows endless,
The night restless.

Let it be,
Waiting for the tribulation to ease.
The body begins to shake,
Frustration quakes.

This is the end,
Tribulation wins.
Who wins,
When living is a sin.

Horizon

The horizon
I can see.
The heavens rain down,
Hope washes over me.
A new day,
Freedom has come.
The heavens rein down,
Faith washes over me.
My eyes open,
Tomorrow
I can see.
The heavens rein down,
A new day,
A beautiful thing,
The horizon,
I can see.

Silent Grave

A grave
With just a name
No birth date,
No death date
Not even a year.
A mysterious aura,
Draws mw near.
A story yearning to be told,
Calling from an unknown grave.
A grave
With just a name.
An image appears,
The person they use to be,
The vision is near.
A family blood line
Becomes clear.
Unsolved tale,
A story yearning to be told.
Silent
The image lingers in front of me.
A grave
With just a name.

Borderline

Condemn
I was told today.
No hope for me,
Lock me up throw away the key.
I feel perfectly fine,
I am Borderline.
Condemn
I was told today.
I feel perfectly fine,
The mind begins to shine.
Tomorrow is another day,
Depression will come to stay.
I try to comprehend,
A disorder I can not defend.
I am who I am,
I want it no other way.
Condemn
I was today.
Anxiety takes flight,
I will fight.
Giving in,
I will not let myself win.
No hope for me,
Lock me up throw away the key.
Condemn
I was told today.

One Direction

You look,
I look away.
Two separate directions,
Leading one way.

Thoughts are unsaid,
An expression is the soul.
Leaving I dread,
When one is not whole.

One direction,
Leading one way.
I look,
You look away.

Two hundred poems

Two hundred unpublished poems,
Not sure what to do.
Collect dust as they sit at home,
Send them to be published,
Maybe the book will come through.

Two hundred poems,
Published art could be so near.
Do I send them,
Or,
Keep them for one more year.

Two hundred poems
Courage is my only defense,
I will keep them
Tucked away safe at home.
Rejection is to intense.

Feline Eyes

Curious is the glance,
Silent is the steps,
Black coat
Shiny and sleek.
Away with the pest.
Green eyes gaze,
Glancing my way.
A face the creature makes,
Lost in a daze,
Slowly it begins to quake.

I Lay upon the Sand

I lay upon the sand
I hear a chuckle,
I become lost in thought.
Raw
Is the texture
Below my hands.
Scent of salt,
Crystals in my palms.
The breeze,
Makes the day feel calm.
Blue waves
Kiss the shore.
Time finds me,
Wasting the day.
Ecstasy,
Is found upon sandy shores.
I lay upon the sand.

Failure

A failure,
I was meant to be.
An illness,
A normal life,
This I will never see.
An illness,
Not one,
But two.
A failure,
I was meant to be.
Safe,
Locked away behind a door,
Safe,
My thoughts are from the world.
Try,
I will not succeed,
A failure,
I was meant to be.

Permanent

I look into the mirror,
Vanity is what I see.
A deceived reflection,
I don't like me.
With dissatisfaction,
A face grows old.
Another wrinkle
Adds distraction,
Aging is a permanent mold.

Untitled XX

Dark eyes
In my sight.
Cocooned in a blanket of warmth,
I feel your skin.
Under the covers,
Safe and warm.
I smell your scent,
Love is pure.

The Righteous

I have been judged
Without a reason.
I have been criticized
By the innocent.
I have been condemned
Before I could succeed.
My wings have been broken,
Before I could fly.
I have been condemned
Without a say.
I have been criticized,
No chance for improvement.
I have been judged,
By the righteous today.

The Past Unfolds

Stories are told,
The past unfolds.
I hear the bells toll,
Familiar voices grow old.
Moonless night,
Disturbing night.
The truth is said,
The story I dread.
Youth is bitter and sweet.
On a moonless night age is complete.
I hear the bell toll,
Familiar voices grow old.
The past unfolds,
Stories are told.

Sleepless Dawn

Insomnia finds me
Dawn approaches.
Light of day sets me free,
The dew falls all around me.

Another day is here,
I watch the robins fly,
The morning sun lights up the night sky,
I believe sleep is near.

Rays of gold,
Rays of red.
Morpheus I yearn to hold,
Sleepless dawn I find instead.

Rest is no where near,
Another sleepless dawn is here.
Light of dawn set me free,
Insomnia finds me.

A Memory of Kisses

A good-bye wave,
Blowing kisses.
He looks back,
Standing at the door,
A tiny person,
His little girl.
He walks away,
Carrying her memory.
Searching for hope
A better life
One that is made for her.
Love is found,
Within the loneliest of hearts.
Distance he travels,
Every journey made.
A memory carries,
Blowing kisses,
A good-bye wave.

Fate leads me to You

Chance draws a line,
Love is time.
Loving you is my solitude,
Fate leads me to you.

Journey I have crossed,
Roads have been lost.
My burden to carry,
These feelings I ill never burry.

A second chance god has given,
My feelings no longer remain hidden.
Loving you is my solitude,
Fate leads me to you.

Dimension of Time

Forever
Dimension of time,
A long parallel.
No life,
No death,
No meaning,
No existents.
A long parallel,
Dimension of time,
Forever.

The End

The end is near,
This I fear.
Relief for some,
While others are undone.

The end is near,
This I fear,
The time is past,
This is over at last.

The end is near,
This I fear.
Our time is over,
Time for closer.

The end is near,
This I fear,
Relief for some,
While others are undone.